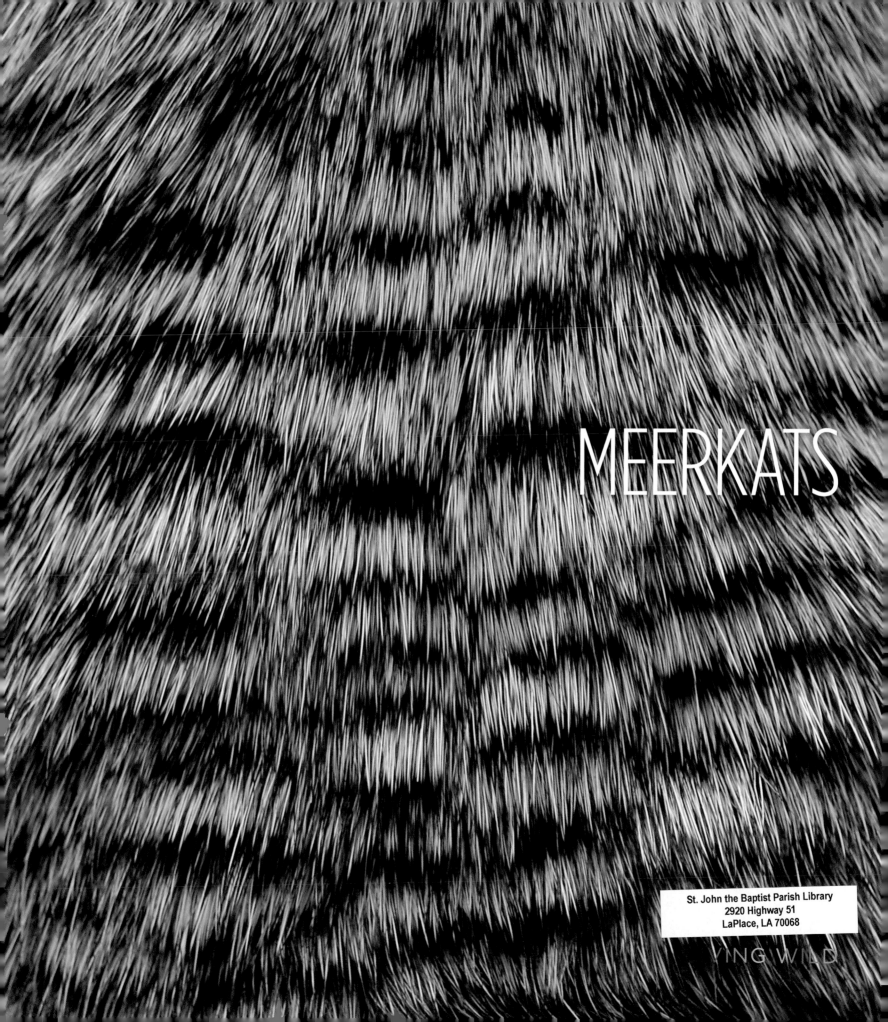

MEERKATS

LIVING WILD

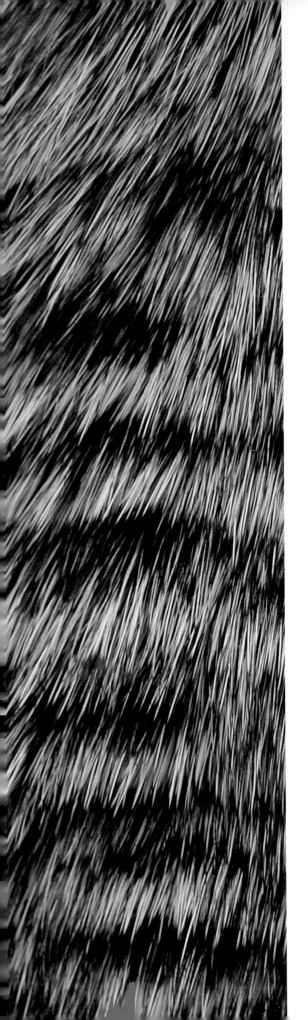

LIVING WILD

Published by Creative Education and Creative Paperbacks
P.O. Box 227, Mankato, Minnesota 56002
Creative Education and Creative Paperbacks are imprints of The Creative Company
www.thecreativecompany.us

Design and production by Mary Herrmann
Art direction by Rita Marshall
Printed in Malaysia

Photographs by Alamy (AF archive, AfriPics.com, FLPA, GLS, John Warburton-Lee Photography, Photoshot Holdings Ltd), Corbis (Theo Allofs/CORBIS, Pete Oxford/ Minden Pictures, Radius Images, Paul Souders, Niels van Gijn/JAI, Michael Weber/ imageBROKER), Creative Commons Wikimedia (Júlio Reis), Dreamstime (Charlotte Leaper), iStockphoto (kmwphotography), Landov (MATTHEW TABACCOS/Barcroft Media), Shutterstock (24Novembers, AndreAnita, Arsgera, chert28, CraigBurrows, Grobler du Preez, EcoPrint, Elle1, gracious_tiger, KAMONRAT, Robert Koss, SARIN KUNTHONG, Michael Maes, Momo5287, Chris Moody, Nasared, Alta Oosthuizen, PhotoSky, Pyty, Romas_Photo, Javier Soto Vazquez, Super Prin, Robert Taylor, Aleksandar Todorovic, Mogens Trolle, PeterVrabel)

Library of Congress Cataloging-in-Publication Data
Gish, Melissa.
Meerkats / Melissa Gish.
p. cm. — (Living wild)
Includes bibliographical references and index.
Summary: A look at meerkats, including their habitats, physical characteristics such as their tails, behaviors, relationships with humans, and their stable status in the world today.
ISBN 978-1-60818-569-6 (hardcover)
ISBN 978-1-62832-170-8 (pbk)
1. Meerkat—Juvenile literature. 2. Rare mammals—Juvenile literature. I. Title.

QL737.C235G57 2015
599.74'2—dc23   2014028011

CCSS: RI.5.1, 2, 3, 8; RST.6–8.1, 2, 5, 6, 8; RH.6–8.3, 4, 5, 6, 7, 8

First Edition HC 9 8 7 6 5 4 3 2 1
First Edition PBK 9 8 7 6 5 4 3 2 1

CREATIVE EDUCATION • CREATIVE PAPERBACKS

MEERKATS

Melissa Gish

In Botswana's Central Kalahari Game Reserve, a meerkat emerges from a dusty hole. She looks in every

direction as she races from one bush to another,
nabbing fat grasshoppers from the thorny branches.

In Botswana's Central Kalahari Game Reserve, the relentless sun scorches the grass and bakes the earth. A meerkat emerges from a dusty hole. She looks in every direction as she races from one bush to another, nabbing fat grasshoppers from the thorny branches. She carries the squirming creatures back to the hole and drops them to the ground, quickly covering them with her front feet to halt their escape. She chirps, and three young meerkats, her younger siblings, emerge from the hole. They jump and roll about excitedly, eager for breakfast. The adult meerkat lifts her paws, releasing the grasshoppers. The young meerkats pounce. One grasshopper tries to spring away, but the adult tosses it back into the skirmish. Learning how to capture prey is one of the first lessons of meerkat life. Suddenly, a martial eagle screeches overhead, and the meerkats dive back into their burrow. Avoiding predators is a meerkat's second lesson.

WHERE IN THE WORLD THEY LIVE

■ *Suricata suricatta siricata*
South Africa, Botswana, Zimbabwe, and Mozambique

■ *Suricata suricatta majoriae*
Namibia

■ *Suricata suricatta iona*
Angola and Zambia

The three meerkat subspecies all make their homes in the deserts or grasslands of southern Africa, ranging from Angola to South Africa. Meerkats are well known for their social nature, which allows them to live in community with one another. The colored squares on this page represent the countries in which meerkats can be found today.

DESERT WARRIORS

Southern Africa's yellow mongoose sometimes shares its scrubland or grassland home with its meerkat cousins.

Meerkats are the only species in the genus *Suricata* of the mongoose family Herpestidae. They make their homes in the sun-scorched scrublands of the Kalahari and Namib deserts —two of Africa's hottest places. One meerkat subspecies is found in Angola and Zambia; a second inhabits Namibia; and a third lives in South Africa, Botswana, and Zimbabwe. The word "meerkat" did not originally describe meerkats at all. Seventeenth-century Dutch merchants used the words *meer* (meaning "sea") and *kat* (meaning "cat") to describe the small, long-tailed monkeys they encountered in their travels to Asia. When the Dutch arrived in southern Africa a century later, they used the same words to describe the small animals they encountered on the fringes of the desert where they collected slaves for the Dutch East India Company. The name stuck, and no one ever offered a more scientific one to replace it.

Of the more than 30 species belonging to the mongoose family, the meerkat is the only one that is not a true mongoose. Like its mongoose relatives, the meerkat is a small, agile, meat-eating **mammal** that lives

Young meerkats learn how to bite off a scorpion's stinger before the creature can deliver its deadly venom.

Meerkats drink very little water, instead getting moisture from the roots, plants, and prey they eat.

in underground burrows. Both mongooses and meerkats are known for their fearlessness of snakes. However, the meerkat differs from its mongoose cousins in a number of ways. Mongooses have bushy tails and are generally nocturnal, meaning they are active at night. They typically live and hunt alone or in pairs, eating birds, rodents, lizards, snakes, and eggs. Meerkats have sticklike tails and are active during the day. They live in family groups, called mobs or gangs, consisting of up to 40 members. Meerkats prey largely on insects—particularly large grasshoppers and beetles—as well as **larvae** and worms. They will also eat small lizards and rodents if available and plant roots and fruit, if extra moisture is needed. And while most animals steer clear of **venomous** scorpions, meerkats attack and eat them with vigor.

Meerkats are 10 to 14 inches (25.4–35.6 cm) long, and their stiff tail adds another 7 to 10 inches (17.8–25.4 cm). They often stand on their hind legs to survey their surroundings, using the tail as a prop for balance. Meerkats weigh less than two pounds (0.9 kg) on average and have brownish-gray fur with dark stripes on their backs. Each meerkat has a different stripe pattern. They

Living in a mob enables meerkats to increase their survival chances amidst the harsh conditions of the Kalahari.

Sharp claws, invisible eyelids, and closable ears are characteristics that allow meerkats to be supreme desert burrowers.

have strong legs and are capable of sprinting up to 20 miles (32.2 km) per hour. The bottoms of meerkats' feet are completely covered with thick, black pads, and each paw has four clawed toes used for digging, climbing, and holding down prey. Front claws are nearly one inch (2.5 cm) long. While meerkats may scratch at prey or enemies with their claws, they mostly use their teeth as weapons. Meerkats have 2 pairs of canines and 6 pairs of incisors, which easily pierce and tear apart the hard **carapaces** of their prey, and up to 12 pairs of grinding teeth.

Living in the desert, meerkats are often subjected to high winds and blowing sand. And as burrowing animals, they are constantly throwing sand into their own faces. See-through inner eyelids called nictitating (*NIK-tih-tayt-ing*) membranes protect their eyes, and muscles in the ears pinch shut to keep sand out. Meerkats have exceptional distance vision. They can spot a predatory bird in the sky from more than half a mile (0.8 km) away. The dark circles around their eyes reflect light and serve to cut the desert sun's glare, while their horizontal **pupils** provide keen depth perception. At close range, though, meerkat vision is slightly blurry. Meerkats make up for this with their sharp

Dung beetles roll meerkat feces into balls upon which they lay eggs that will hatch into dung-eating larvae.

Like dogs and other scent markers, meerkats lift their hind leg higher when trying to replace other scents.

sense of smell. They can smell prey underground and can even tell if a predator or rival meerkat has been nearby. Meerkats have glands on their cheeks and anal region that emit musk, a greasy substance with an odor specific to each animal. They mark their territory, called a home range, by rubbing on rocks and trees, and they may also use feces, urine, or saliva to let other meerkat mobs know that the land is occupied. They even rub their musk on each other. Scent recognition helps meerkats bond and signals when mating should take place.

Meerkats have no fat reserves, so they must forage for food daily. They may travel up to two miles (3.2 km) per day in search of prey. Deserts are commonly believed to be hot all the time, but this is not always the case. In Africa's southern deserts, daytime temperatures can reach 160 °F (71.1 °C) in the sun and 100 °F (37.8 °C) in the shade. But when the sun goes down, temperatures average just 40 to 50 °F (4.4 to 10 °C), and during the winter months of July through September, the overnight temperature can drop below 0 °F (–17.8 °C). Emerging from their burrows in the morning, meerkats stand on their hind legs and face the sun. Their bellies have a

Meerkats warm up quickly as they greet the morning sun, readying their bodies for the day's activities.

Youngsters at play learn valuable social skills that will later help them perform their duties within the mob.

nearly hairless patch that allows their black skin to soak up the sun's rays, warming their bodies and energizing them for a day of foraging. As the sun begins to set in the evening, the meerkats repeat this ritual, heating up for the long, chilly night to come, before crowding together in their burrow.

Slender and yellow mongooses share the meerkat's desert habitat, but because their diets differ, they do not compete for food. Yellow mongooses will eat meerkat babies, called pups, but during the time of year when there are no small pups in the meerkat mob, meerkats allow yellow mongooses, as well as ground squirrels, to live among the mob and share their burrows. The meerkats and their neighbors participate equally in the tasks of watching for predators, keeping the burrow clean, and chasing out unwelcome snakes that commonly seek shelter from the sweltering desert heat. The Cape cobra and the puff adder, two of Africa's most venomous snakes, also often prey upon meerkat pups. However, when faced with an entire mob of meerkats jumping and biting in fierce defense, even the most fearsome snake typically races away from the scene.

About 50 subspecies of slender mongoose are commonly found throughout central and southern Africa.

Burrows can be up to 16 feet (4.9 m) long and contain multiple tunnels and rooms for sleeping.

Constantly on the alert for danger, meerkats stay close together when not foraging on their own.

MOBS OF MEERKATS

Meerkats spend their days foraging, napping, grooming, and playing. Picking fleas and ticks out of each other's fur not only helps meerkats remain healthy but also secures bonds among members of the mob. Young meerkats play together to develop their agility and hunting skills, while older meerkats play-fight to teach younger meerkats defense strategies. Play-fighting also maintains the **hierarchy** of the mob. In addition, meerkats spend time cleaning and repairing their elaborate system of tunnels and burrows hidden underground. Meerkats may dig their own burrows, but they are more likely to take over the abandoned burrows of other animals and make them part of the mob's system. Dozens of entrances to the tunnels are maintained throughout a meerkat home range, which varies from about 0.3 to 1.2 square miles (0.8–3.1 sq km) in size. In addition, many small tunnels called bolt holes are dug to provide a place to escape predators. Wherever meerkats are foraging, they tend to stray no more than 50 feet (15.2 m) from each other or from a bolt hole.

A meerkat mob will defend its territory from intruders such as neighboring mobs looking to expand their territory

Meerkats are so wary of birds of prey that an airplane flying overhead will often send them running for cover.

Meerkats are one of the few mammals that take turns doing different jobs, including babysitting.

or males that stray from their own mob to mate with females in another mob. Usually, a fierce display of teeth and claws combined with loud vocalizations will be enough to deter intruders. However, if resources are limited and a neighboring mob is desperate for new foraging land, meerkats will fight to control territory. A stronger mob may take over a territory, displacing its occupants.

In meerkat society, a mob is led by a dominant male and female, called an alpha pair. Other members of the mob are the pair's offspring and, on rare occasions, one or more stray meerkats that were allowed to join the mob. Every meerkat knows its place in the mob's hierarchy. The alpha female, usually the oldest and only one allowed to deliver offspring, is called the matriarch. Older siblings that watch over pups are called babysitters, and meerkats that partner with juveniles to teach them necessary skills are called mentors.

A sentry, or lookout, is responsible for staying alert to predators and for warning the rest of the mob when danger approaches. Meerkats take turns standing guard. After a good meal, and with a full stomach, a meerkat gives up foraging to do nothing but constantly scan the horizon and look skyward for any sign of danger. The meerkats' greatest threat comes from above. Martial eagles, with razor-sharp talons and wingspans greater than six feet (1.8 m), regularly patrol meerkat ranges. Sentries continuously stand on their hind legs. When all is well, they vocalize a pattern of chirps to keep the mob calm and focused on their task of foraging. But when sentries spot eagles, they burst into loud barks. The mob then races for burrow entrances. Recent research

The role of sentry is the most important job in a meerkat mob—and often the most dangerous.

The highly aggressive puff adder is responsible for most human snakebite fatalities in Africa.

While mongooses eat snakes, meerkats must battle them to protect the mob, biting at them until they leave.

conducted by **behavioral ecologists** at Cambridge University in England has revealed that meerkats actually fight over the opportunity to stand guard. The research suggests that meerkats recognize that their role as a sentry allows them to be the first to see danger and thus the first to respond by running for safety. In more than 2,000 hours of observations, the research team did not record the loss of a single sentry to predators.

In the wild, dangers from predators, diseases such as bovine tuberculosis and rabies, and starvation claim many meerkats' lives. Only 1 in 4 pups survives to adulthood, but those that do can live as long as 10 years. Captive meerkats can live up to 15 years. Meerkats are old enough to mate at about 10 months of age. Reproduction is highly structured to maintain the **genetic** health of the mob. When the alpha female is ready to mate, she will chase away all other mature females, forcing them to either wander alone or band together in a smaller group for a time. Only the alpha male and alpha female will mate with each other. Sometimes, while she is out foraging, the alpha female will mate with a stray male that sneaks into the territory. Related meerkats will never

Meerkats enhance relationships with mob members by touching one another and grooming each other's fur.

Meerkats seem to trust and respect the leader of their mob and will follow her rules.

mate with each other. After the alpha female has given birth, the other mature females are allowed to return to the mob. Most do, but some join other mobs or gather with stray males to form new mobs.

While they are cast out of the mob, some females will mate with stray males and become pregnant. Usually, they do not deliver babies, but if they do, they may try to sneak the babies back into the mob after the alpha female has given birth. If the alpha female notices the babies, she will kill them so that only her babies survive to become part of the family group. Only about one in five babies is successfully sneaked into a mob.

Meerkats can breed up to four times a year. After a **gestation** period of 70 days, up to 6 pups are born hairless and blind. They weigh just one ounce (28.3 g). For the first two to three weeks, they remain inside the burrow, feeding on their mother's milk. Then, they venture outside the burrow. When not feeding on milk, the pups remain under the constant supervision of babysitters. At four weeks old, the pups begin to follow babysitters around, watching them forage and begging for food, which the babysitters provide. Within two more weeks, they begin foraging for their own food. Depending on the availability of prey, the pups' babysitters may still help them catch food, and their mother may still supply milk for up to 10 more weeks. Once fully **weaned**, each pup is taken under the guidance of a mentor. Mentors teach pups how to disarm scorpions, defend against snake attacks, and respond to alarm calls, among other survival skills. At two to three years of age, most males and some females leave their families to form new mobs.

Because they are ever alert to potential danger, meerkat mothers often nurse their young while standing on their hind legs.

horus

When predators are known to be in the area, sentries may double up to cover every possible angle.

HEARTS OF GOLD

Meerkats are some of the most popular attractions for people who visit South Africa on wildlife tours. And now, meerkats are worth their weight in gold—almost. Each year, the South African Mint Company releases a set of pure gold collector coins that highlight the country's wildlife. In 2011, meerkats were the featured animals. On the 0.1-ounce (2.8 g) coin, a meerkat rests on a tree branch, and on the 0.25-ounce (7.1 g) coin, an alpha male stands guard as an alpha female grooms a pup. The 0.5-ounce (14.2 g) coin features a sentry, while the one-ounce (28.3 g) coin depicts a family of eight watchful meerkats. Because only a limited number of the meerkat coins were made, they are now valued at several thousand dollars by collectors.

Meerkats were valued long before people collected them on coins. In the **mythology** of Zambia and Zimbabwe, meerkats came to be called sun angels. A sun angel was believed to keep away moon devils, or a type of werewolf creature. It was also believed that sun angels would protect people who were lost in the wilderness and help guide them home. Today, meerkats are still thought

In a meerkat mob, protecting the young is the highest priority because it ensures the group's long-term success.

A meerkat relies on its sense of smell to detect food that may be too close for its eyes to see.

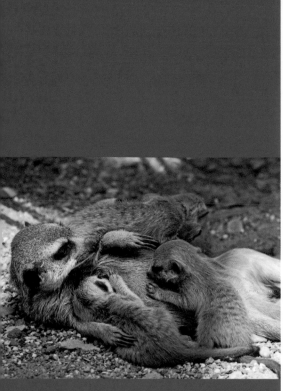

Though meerkat mothers can nurse standing up, they take every available opportunity to rest with their young.

The Kalahari Meerkat Project has found that pups with the loudest begging cries receive the most food from babysitters.

to bring good fortune if seen. A meerkat crossing your path is especially lucky because meerkats are scarce in Zambia and Zimbabwe, living only in the corners of the Kalahari Desert that reach into those countries.

The **indigenous** people of southern Africa, known as the San, include many stories about mongooses and meerkats in their traditional folklore. One story tells of a mongoose that used a spear to hunt an eland, a species of antelope. The mongoose speared the eland, which ran away and then died. Before the mongoose could track its prize, a group of meerkats came upon the eland carcass and began carving it up to carry back to their burrows. When the mongoose arrived at the scene, he began arguing with the meerkats over the kill. The argument raged all day and night until the mongoose became so frustrated that it ran away and let the meerkats have all the meat. In reality, neither mongooses nor meerkats typically choose to eat **carrion**. However, in times of drought, when prey burrow much deeper in the ground than normal and foraging becomes difficult, both mongooses and meerkats will eat carrion.

For generations, meerkats have played a role in the **cultural** heritage of South Africa, but these little animals

have become popular the world over in recent decades, thanks to television and movies. The 1994 Disney animated film *The Lion King* introduced the world to Timon the meerkat and his best friend, a warthog named Pumbaa. Timon has a joke for every situation. His carefree attitude is best expressed by the words "Hakuna Matata," which he sings with Pumbaa. In Swahili, a language spoken by a large portion of southeastern Africa's population, the phrase means "no worries." The popularity of Timon and Pumbaa led to further appearances in the

After Timon and Pumbaa save Simba's life, the three become friends and have many adventures together.

RIKKI-TIKKI-TAVI

If you read the old books of natural history, you will find they say that when the mongoose fights the snake and happens to get bitten, he runs off and eats some herb that cures him. That is not true. The victory is only a matter of quickness of eye and quickness of foot—snake's blow against mongoose's jump—and as no eye can follow the motion of a snake's head when it strikes, this makes things much more wonderful than any magic herb. Rikki-tikki knew he was a young mongoose, and it made him all the more pleased to think that he had managed to escape a blow from behind. It gave him confidence in himself, and when Teddy came running down the path, Rikki-tikki was ready to be petted.

from The Jungle Book, by Rudyard Kipling (1865–1936)

two *Lion King* movie sequels and a weekly television show called *The Lion King's Timon & Pumbaa*, which ran from 1995 to 1999. The meerkat and warthog duo also made regular appearances on *Disney's House of Mouse*, a cable show that ran from 2001 to 2002. In addition, from 2008 to 2013, eight short films were produced for a series called *Wild About Safety: Safety Smart with Timon and Pumbaa*. The films offered safety tips on a variety of issues, including fire, water, and even the Internet.

An entire community of real-life meerkats was captured on film from 2005 to 2008, when Animal Planet presented the highly popular weekly show *Meerkat Manor*. Part documentary and part dramatic storytelling, the show was the first of its kind to follow real animals through months of struggles and successes in the wild. As subjects of research conducted by the Kalahari Meerkat Project, a number of different meerkat mobs were featured on *Meerkat Manor*. The main characters were members of the Whiskers mob, led for the first two and a half seasons by a matriarch named Flower. During the third season of *Meerkat Manor*, Flower suffered a fatal snakebite and was replaced by a female offspring named Rocket Dog. British

Because meerkats can lose up to 5 percent of their body weight overnight, they must find food first thing in the morning.

Zinzi and Bob were inseparable pals for the first few months of Zinzi's life at Predator World.

All members of a meerkat mob use a common area away from sleeping and eating areas as a bathroom.

zoologist Tim Clutton-Brock's 2008 book *Meerkat Manor: Flower of the Kalahari* retold Flower's life story.

In addition to the Whiskers mob, other groups of meerkats as well as other types of animals were featured on *Meerkat Manor*. Battles with deadly snakes, fights with other meerkat mobs over territory, and the births of meerkat pups were just some of the highlights of the show. After the series ended, a full-length movie recounted Flower's early years, from her life as a young meerkat to her rise in the ranks that ultimately led to her leadership of the mob. The movie, *Meerkat Manor: The Story Begins*, was shown on Animal Planet in 2008. Today, meerkat fans can watch *Meerkat Manor* on DVD and streaming video.

A meerkat named Bob made international news in 2010 when he was photographed snuggling a lioness cub named Zinzi at Predator World, a zoological reserve in South Africa. As a pup, Bob was rejected by his mother, so a keeper at Predator World took Bob in and raised him. Rather than return to the meerkat mob, Bob remained with his keeper, accepting her as his new family and protecting her like he would a meerkat mob.

Bob would forage on his own during the day but would always return to his keeper to be taken home for the night. Bob met Zinzi the lioness cub when she, too, was rejected by her mother and had to be raised at Predator World. Bob took on the role of playmate and protector, cuddling up with Zinzi at naptime. By the time Zinzi was about three months old, she was too big to safely interact with Bob, so the two friends had to part ways and form new relationships.

As human populations grow, meerkats must become accustomed to sharing their territory with people.

Separating Zimbabwe and South Africa, the Limpopo River forms a floodplain rich with vegetation and wildlife.

KEEPING MEERKATS WILD

The earliest ancestors of meerkats were actually a group of catlike mammals called miacids that emerged around 60 million years ago and existed relatively unchanged for about 30 million years. As miacids spread to new areas, they began to evolve, or change, into different groups of animals specifically suited to their environments. Some became hyenas that roamed grasslands, while others became civets that hunted in the dense forests. Still others became mongooses. Prehistoric mongooses were much larger than modern mongooses, though everything else about them has remained basically the same over the millennia.

By about 11 million years ago, the first modern mongoose (the slender mongoose) evolved. Other modern mongooses soon followed, including the banded mongoose. Some members of this species later evolved into animals suited for life in the dry grasslands: meerkats. The first meerkat was *Suricata suricatta major*. It looked just like today's meerkats, except it was larger and had poorer vision. Fossil remains of this species have been found in the Cave of Hearths, a protected historical site in the Limpopo province

Meerkats dig burrows in compacted soil that will not collapse and forage in soft soil that easily falls apart.

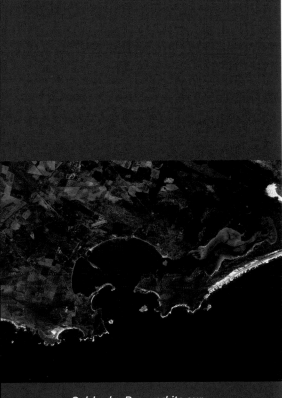

Saldanha Bay and its surrounding area are abundant with the fossils of early plant and animal species.

Annual rainfall in the Kalahari Desert typically ranges from 5 to 20 inches (12.7–50.8 cm), depending on the area.

of South Africa, and in the limestone quarries near Saldanha Bay on the southwestern tip of South Africa. The fossils date to about 2.5 million years ago. As the climate changed to become drier and hotter, this early meerkat became smaller and more agile, and its vision improved, making it perfectly suited to life in the desert.

Today, meerkats enjoy stable populations throughout their native habitats. However, they are vulnerable to changes in their environments caused by **climate change** and human activities. As weather patterns on our planet change, longer periods of little rainfall occur, making the struggle for survival more challenging for meerkats and other desert wildlife. And as humans continue to invade meerkat habitat, meerkat mortality rises. Forced to cross roads while foraging, meerkats risk getting hit by vehicles. As agriculture moves closer to meerkat habitat, meerkats may have to eat insect prey sprayed with pesticides, which can be deadly. In addition, as the popularity of meerkats grows, these animals fall victim to the pet trade.

A 2013 study led by University of Zurich evolutionary biologist Dr. Simon W. Townsend and social sciences engineer Dr. Nicolas Perony found that the introduction

of roads into meerkat territory has changed one of their most unique behaviors. Normally, when meerkats move from place to place to forage, they travel in a group led by the alpha female. However, results of the study indicated that the alpha female would stop when she encountered a road and make one of the lower-ranking meerkats go first. Townsend believes that this **adaptation** occurred to protect the alpha female, since leaders crossing a road are more likely than followers to be killed. The researchers explained that, although it may appear selfish on the part of the alpha female to push one of her offspring toward

The popularity of meerkat TV shows and movies has made the animals top wildlife tourist attractions.

Meerkats are able to distinguish between the intruders in their territory who pose a threat and those who do not.

potential traffic, she seemed to know that her value to the mob as a whole outweighed the life of a single lower-ranking meerkat.

While meerkats have been able to adapt to some of the effects of human activity, they still have little defense when it comes to agricultural expansion. Meerkat burrows are destroyed in order to plant crops, and toxic chemicals are sprayed on the land to kill insects and larvae—the foods that meerkats need to survive. The introduction of cattle and other livestock also ruins meerkat habitat. When large animals trample over land, the soil becomes harder and more compact. Vegetation needed by meerkat prey such as caterpillars and insects is also destroyed. Digging in such hard soil costs meerkats more energy, and they find less prey, which can lead to starvation.

Unlike many wild animals, meerkats are largely unprotected from the pet trade because they are not considered an endangered species. Despite appearing friendly and playful on television, meerkats are still wild animals. James Honeyborne, director of the movie *The Meerkats*, has stressed to the public that meerkats do not make good pets. They climb and explore, so they cannot be kept confined in a cage or even inside a whole house without trying to escape. They constantly dig and chew, so they will tear up carpet and ruin walls, furniture, and anything else they get their paws on. They also smell terrible. Just as in the wild, they mark their boundaries inside a house with musk and urine. Even with proper housing, meerkats need a special diet. Many foods can be deadly to meerkats. Because they live in family groups, keeping them isolated makes them stressed, which can cause them to bite and scratch their owners. Calm,

Because meerkats thrive in groups, keeping a single meerkat as a pet can be harmful to the animal.

Meerkats are naturally curious about humans and have been known to adopt keepers as members of their mob.

adorable meerkats sold as pups behave very differently once they grow up, prompting many owners to abandon or **euthanize** their pets.

Only professional facilities should keep captive meerkats. On the island of Jersey, off the coast of France, the Durrell Wildlife Park raises meerkats. The park wants to practice and perfect techniques that can later be used to **captive-breed** the narrow-striped mongoose, an endangered species from Madagascar that desperately needs help to avoid **extinction**. In 1989, the Fellow Earthlings' Wildlife Center in California became the only privately licensed facility in North America to specialize in meerkats. The staff cares for orphaned, old, sick, and injured meerkats as well as abandoned pet meerkats. The facility, founded by Pam Bennett-Wallberg, is funded by donations, an adopt-a-meerkat program, and private tours.

To help educate the public about meerkats and support research on these animals, the Kalahari Meerkat Project began in 1993 at the Kuruman River Reserve, located near South Africa's border with Botswana. Led by Tim Clutton-Brock, the project studies meerkat behavior and keeps genetic records. The project also assists individuals

and groups with research and presentations, including the production of the National Geographic special *Walking with Meerkats: Meerkat Madness* (2001), an episode of the BBC series *The Life of Mammals* (2002), the 2003 movie *Meerkats*, and the Animal Planet series *Meerkat Manor* (2005–08). While meerkats exist in healthy numbers, they are challenged by the many changes occurring in their environments. Continued research and education on the needs and habits of meerkats is essential to keeping these animals firmly woven into the desert's web of life.

The Durrell Wildlife Park is part of a charitable organization founded in 1963 by naturalist and author Gerald Durrell.

ANIMAL TALE: MEERKATS PAINT THE ANIMALS

The culture of the Venda people of Limpopo (South Africa's northernmost province) is closely tied to wildlife. Although meerkats are typically desert creatures, some meerkats can be found in the Limpopo floodplains. The following myth tells how meerkats in this habitat inspired trust in their animal neighbors.

Long ago, none of the birds or other animals in the Limpopo had any color. Only the meerkats looked different. This was because they were magical creatures a long way from their normal desert habitat to the east. Everyone liked the meerkats, for they knew that these animals always told the truth. Meerkats were fair in their judgments, and they were always willing to share their food.

One day, the birds and other animals gathered at the meerkat village and asked the chief of the meerkats to help them. "Can you use your magic and paint us different colors?" they asked.

"Why me?" questioned the meerkat chief.

"Because," the animals explained, "we trust that you will be wise in this matter."

The meerkat chief agreed. "And afterward," he said, "we will have a great feast to celebrate. To begin, each of you must bring food to share with everyone." The birds flew and the animals ran away in different directions to search for food, while the meerkat chief prepared his magic paintbrush.

After some time, the fishing owl returned from the north. He dropped some plump frogs before the meerkat chief. The frogs were covered with mud. The meerkat chief dipped his paintbrush in the mud and painted the fishing owl's breast with dark speckles. "How fine you look," the chief said. The fishing owl was pleased.

Next, the crocodile arrived from the west with shellfish he'd dug out of the muddy riverbed. The shellfish were coated with green slime. The meerkat chief dipped his brush in the slime and painted the crocodile green. The crocodile was thrilled with his new color.

Presently, the greater kudu returned from the south, carrying tender branches on his back. "These will be delicious," the greater kudu told the meerkat chief, dropping the branches. The chief agreed. Then he used his magic to make paint from the pale branches. He painted the kudu's back with white stripes.

From the east came the carmine bee-eater. The little bird struggled to carry a heavy kola nut. When he reached the meerkat village, he dropped the nut to the ground. It burst open, and dozens of bright red seeds fell out. "Wonderful!" exclaimed the meerkat chief. He rubbed his brush on a soft seed and painted the beautiful red color all over the bee-eater's body.

The rest of the animals returned throughout the day. The leopard brought a mouthful of ripe marula fruits. Because the marula were yellow with small flecks of brown, the meerkat chief painted the leopard yellow with brown spots. When the side-striped jackal brought a batch of dusty worms, the chief painted a dusty gray stripe on the jackal's side. And when the African wild dog brought the bones of an antelope, the chief painted white bone-shaped markings on the wild dog's body.

While some of the animals (such as the black mamba, Cape buffalo, and black heron) chose to remain without color, everyone else loved their different colors and marks. That night, all the creatures enjoyed the celebration feast.

GLOSSARY

adaptation – a change in a species that helps it survive in a changed environment

behavioral ecologists – people who study the effects of environmental pressures on the behavior of animals

captive-breed – breed and raise in a place from which escape is not possible

carapaces – the hard upper shells of crustaceans, insects, spiders, and their relatives

carrion – the rotting flesh of an animal

climate change – the gradual increase in Earth's temperature that causes changes in the planet's atmosphere, environments, and long-term weather conditions

cultural – of or relating to particular groups in a society that share behaviors and characteristics that are accepted as normal by that group

euthanize – put a living being to death painlessly

extinction – the act or process of becoming extinct; coming to an end or dying out

feces – waste matter eliminated from the body

genetic – relating to genes, the basic physical units of heredity

gestation – the period of time it takes a baby to develop inside its mother's womb

hierarchy – a system in which people, animals, or things are ranked in importance one above another

indigenous – originating in a particular region or country

larvae – the newly hatched, wingless, often wormlike form of many insects before they become adults

mammal – a warm-blooded animal that has a backbone and hair or fur, gives birth to live young, and produces milk to feed its young

mythology – a collection of myths, or popular, traditional beliefs or stories that explain how something came to be or that are associated with a person or object

pupils – the dark, circular openings in the center of the eyes through which light passes

venomous – capable of injecting poison by a sting or bite

weaned – made the young of a mammal accept food other than by nursing milk

SELECTED BIBLIOGRAPHY

Animal Planet. "Meerkat Manor." http://animal.discovery.com /tv-shows/meerkat-manor.

Clutton-Brock, Tim. *Meerkat Manor: Flower of the Kalahari*. Cape Town: Sunbird, 2007.

Dennis, Nigel, and David Macdonald. *Meerkats*. Cape Town: Struik, 2001.

Honeyborne, James. *The Meerkats*. DVD. London: BBC Films, 2008.

San Diego Zoo. "Animals: Meerkat." http://animals .sandiegozoo.org/animals/meerkat.

Zoo Atlanta. "Meerkat." http://www.zooatlanta.org/home /animals/mammals/meerkat.

Note: Every effort has been made to ensure that any websites listed above were active at the time of publication. However, because of the nature of the Internet, it is impossible to guarantee that these sites will remain active indefinitely or that their contents will not be altered.

Even though meerkats are numerous, they are still vulnerable to the effects of human activities.

INDEX